Time to Tell Time

by Janine Scott

Content and Reading Adviser: Mary Beth Fletcher, Ed.D.
Educational Consultant/Reading Specialist
The Carroll School, Lincoln, Massachusetts

COMPASS POINT BOOKS

Minneapolis, Minnesota

LOCUST VALLEY LIBRARY

Compass Point Books
3109 West 50th Street, #115
Minneapolis, MN 55410

Visit Compass Point Books on the Internet at *www.compasspointbooks.com*
or e-mail your request to *custserv@compasspointbooks.com*

Photographs ©: Phil Bulgasch, cover, 1; Cat Gwynn/Corbis, 4 (left); Ingram Publishing, 4 (right);
Photo Network/Henryk T. Kaiser, 5; Michael Lustbader/The Image Finders, 6; Mark E. Gibson/
The Image Finders, 7; Victoria & Albert Museum, London/Art Resource, N.Y., 8; Joseph Sohm/
ChromoSohm Inc./Corbis, 9; Bettmann/Corbis, 10; Eric R. Berndt/The Image Finders, 11;
Giansanti Gianni/Corbis Sygma, 12; Hulton/Archive by Getty Images, 13, 15; Stock Montage, 14;
John Van Hasselt/Corbis Sygma, 17; Randy Miller/Corbis, 18; Jim Baron/The Image Finders, 19.

Project Manager: Rebecca Weber McEwen
Editors: Heidi Schoof and Patricia Stockland
Photo Researcher: Svetlana Zhurkina
Designer: Jaime Martens
Illustrator: Anna-Maria Crum

Library of Congress Cataloging-in-Publication Data
Scott, Janine.   129-8714
 Time to tell time / by Janine Scott.
  p. cm. — (Spyglass books)
 Includes bibliographical references and index.
 Contents: What's the time?—Nature and time—The solar clock—
Early timekeepers—Early clocks—Time around the world—
Keeping time in line—Time for fun—Time flies!
 ISBN 0-7565-0455-4 (hardcover)
 1. Time—Juvenile literature.   [1. Time. 2. Time measurements.]   I. Title. II. Series.
  QB209.5.S375 2003
  529—dc21   2002012630

© 2003 by Compass Point Books
All rights reserved. No part of this book may be reproduced without written permission from the
publisher. The publisher takes no responsibility for the use of any of the materials or methods
described in this book, nor for the products thereof.
Printed in the United States of America.

Contents

NOTE: Glossary words are in **bold** the first time they appear.

Telling Time

What time is it? Is it time to get up, time to go to school, or time to catch a bus?

There are many ways to tell time.

Nature and Time

Long ago, people used nature to tell time.

Day and night helped people measure time.

The changing seasons also helped people measure time.

A Sun Clock

The earliest tool for telling time was the sundial.

A sundial tells time by measuring the shadow the sun makes as it moves across the sky.

People also told time with clocks that used water or sand.

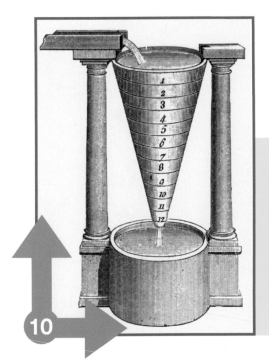

People could tell how much time had passed by measuring how much water or sand had flowed away.

Some early clocks used weights to make the hour hand move.

Windup clocks used *springs* to make the hands move.

12

When people started to travel by train, they needed to know exactly what time it was.

Overnight Between
New York or Boston and Chicago

Save a business day and enjoy a perfect night's rest
over the comfortable "Water Level Route" via the

20th Century Limited

Lv. New York	4.00 P.M.	Lv. Chicago	2.30 P.M.
Lv. Boston	1.30 P.M.	Ar. Boston	11.50 A.M.
Ar. Chicago	8.55 A.M.	Ar. New York	9.25 A.M.

If people did not know the *local time,* they could miss their train.

In 1884 people decided that the world should have *standard time.*

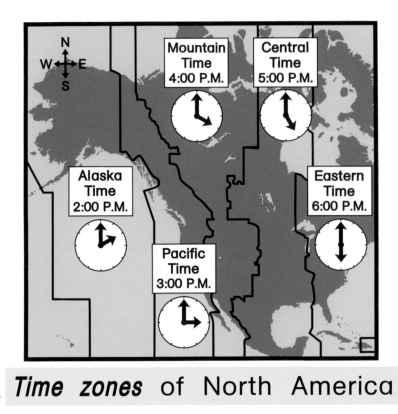

N
W E
S

Mountain
Time
4:00 P.M.

Central
Time
5:00 P.M.

Alaska
Time
2:00 P.M.

Eastern
Time
6:00 P.M.

Pacific
Time
3:00 P.M.

Time zones of North America

In Greenwich, England, people can visit the line that is the starting point for standard time.

Some countries change their clocks so that it stays light later in the evening. This is called *daylight saving time.*

People can use the extra hour of daylight to work or play outside.

18

Fun Facts

At the beginning of daylight saving time, clocks "spring" forward an hour. At the end of daylight saving time, clocks "fall" back an hour.

Greenwich, England, sets the time zones for the rest of the world. This is called Greenwich Mean Time.

ENGLAND

Greenwich

The word "clock" comes from the Latin word "clocca," which means bell. Early clocks rang a bell on the hour.

Sundials don't work on cloudy days or at night!

Glossary

daylight saving time–when clocks are put forward one hour to get more daylight in the evening

local time–the time in a certain place

springs–metal spirals that go back to their original shape after being stretched or pulled

standard time–a way to measure time that is used in most places around the world

time zone–an area of Earth where all places share the same time

Learn More

Books

Holtz, Lara Tankel. *What's the Time?* London; New York: Dorling Kindersley, 2001.

Older, Jules. *Telling Time: How to Tell Time on Digital and Analog Clocks!* Watertown, MA: Charlesbridge Publishing, 2000.

Pistoia, Sara. *Time.* Chanhassen, Minn.: Child's World, 2002.

Web Sites

World Book
http://worldbook.bigchalk.com/150145.htm

Museum of Science and Industry
www.msichicago.org/exhibit/time/educ_pages/act_yourtime.html

Index

GR: I
Word Count: 116

From Janine Scott

I live in New Zealand and have two daughters. They love to read books that are full of fun facts and features. I hope you do, too!

24

LOCUST VALLEY LIBRARY

S 2245 00129 071 4

11-08   1

1-16   1   _____

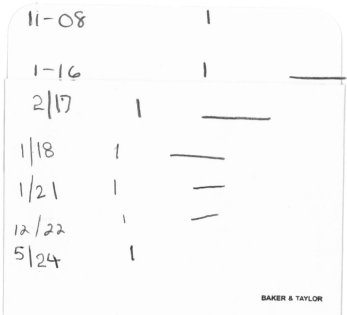

2/17   1   _____

1/18   1   _____

1/21   1   _____

12/22   1   ____

5/24   1

BAKER & TAYLOR